Oliphant!

Bob —
I appreciate your
help!

Ted

Oliphant!

a cartoon collection
by Pat Oliphant

Andrews and McMeel, Inc.
A Universal Press Syndicate Company
Kansas City • New York • Washington

ISBN: 0-8362-6205-0
Library of Congress Catalog Number 79-92212

Foreword

The roisterous comedian W.C. Fields is supposed to have remarked, "Any man who hates children and dogs can't be all bad." I think he would have loved Pat Oliphant.

I once was enjoying a long liquid lunch with Oliphant at our favorite watering hole on Capitol Hill, when a woman with three small children chanced to sit next to us at the bar. More accurately, the children sat down in a great clang and clamor next to Oliphant himself. Well sir, he jumped off his bar stool as if poked with a cattle prod, ran off a safe distance, and began loudly to declaim against children in the aggregate. A quick silence fell and people began to squirm, the woman and her offspring being black. Pat Oliphant drew himself up to the full measure of his indignation and loudly explained: "Lady, I'm not a racist. I'm a **kidist!**" It was Oliphant who proposed solving the energy crisis by melting down all the world's children: "Three kids equal a full barrel of oil, ya know." He later claimed to have been quoting someone else, but some of us had our doubts.

Oliphant's lady friend owns two large dogs. The man of the house constructed an expensive fence to contain them, and no doubt to isolate them from himself. They patiently waited until the fence had been completed, promptly jumped it, chased a pregnant lady down the block, and landed Pat Oliphant in the middle of a lawsuit. This gave him new ammunition against dogs and children as yet even unborn.

Somehow, life seems to work out like that for Pat Oliphant. Perhaps it is such random spills or traumas that permit Oliphant to view the world's absurdities through the mad eye of the cartoonist.

Oliphant is neither a knee-jerk liberal, nor an automatic reactionary. He somehow has a way of coming down all over the ideological lot—and, often, of making **both** sides angry with the same cartoon. My favorite example of this is the single Oliphant work simultaneously sinking darts deeply into Senator Ted Kennedy, the well-known midnight aquanaut, and President Jimmy Carter, the well-known born-again peanut farmer. Here is Kennedy, all knotty jaws and grins, driving a powerful sedan while Carter (wizened and worried in scuba-diving gear) cringes unhappily and impotently in the back seat. It was at once the funniest, and maybe the meanest, political cartoon I have ever seen. I hereby nominate it for a prize no smaller than the Nobel—about the only bauble Oliphant has not yet won. Among his top prizes are the Pulitzer and the cherished award from his colleagues of the National Cartoonist Society.

Though certainly Oliphant gave the Watergate thugs their due licks (Nixon as a rat gnawing through a wall to get at the infamous tapes; John Ehrlichman, in full Nazi storm-trooper gear, pounding the table while he thundered to investigating senators, "We were only

6

obeying orders!"), he also depicted John Dean, who'd blown the whistle on the White House gang, as an exploiting opportunist wearing expensive price-tags representing his rich book and television contracts. Oliphant made Women's Libbers nervous by ridiculing the Girl Scouts of America for refusing males membership at the same time young girls were successfully petitioning to play Little League baseball and their adult counterparts were warring on all-male saloons.

Cartoonists get much mean mail if they are doing their jobs right. Partisans rage not only at the blunt symbols—C.I.A. men as grinning death heads; Henry Kissinger as a smelly fish Uncle Sam is trying to sell the world—but at the efficient way cartoonists reduce complex issues or ideas to the lowest common denominator. I think this is because the good cartoonist has the ability to peel away the protective bark of the human tree, to cut through obtuse or pompous rhetoric, and—having stripped away the stuffings—to toss the bleached bones of reality hard upon the naked beach.

As a sometimes political writer, I often envy such efficient cuttings. The only disagreement I have with the old truism "A picture is worth a thousand words" is that when a cartoonist such as Oliphant takes pen in hand he exposes that old adage as being understated.

One bit of advice to the Oliphant reader: when inspecting his cartoons, don't forget to follow the ancient instructions of photographers dealing with children: "Look at the little birdie."

Here, then, is the latest Oliphant. Enjoy.

—Larry L. King
Washington, D.C.

9

'THIS HASN'T BEEN EASY —— I HOPE IT GETS YOU THROUGH THE WINTER!'

11

A WASHINGTON VARIATION OF THE NATIONAL JOGGING FAD

LIBERALS FOR TAX CUTS

GOP TAX CUT CAMPAIGN

SUPPORT THE TAX BLITZ

READY WITH THE SHOVEL...

13

'YOU WANT A SUIT, I GOT A SUIT––– SO, WHENEVER DID I SAY YOU'D LIKE THE FIT?'

14

'BY GOLLY, YOU'RE RIGHT, MR. SOMOZA — COMMUNISTS EVERYWHERE! I HOPE YOU GOT 'EM ALL'

16

"JIMMY, I DECLARE, IT'S THREE IN THE MORNING! STOP THINKING ABOUT THE POLLS AND GET UP HERE TO BED!"

'GO ASK RAFSHOON IF I'M STRONG ENOUGH IN THE NATIONAL POLLS TO SAY 'NO' TO THE PORK-BARREL ISSUE.'

'REALLY? WELL, IF IT INTERESTS YOU, I DON'T THINK OF <u>YOU</u> AS A PEOPLE'S POPE, EITHER!'

GUIDELINE

21

'HELLO, DERE, YOU LUCKY PEOPLE — ISS DER LONE RANGER BACK VUNCE AGAIN!'

'AREN'T YOU PIGS WONDERFUL?'

24

25

'FERGUSON, WE WANT YOU BACK AT HEADQUARTERS TO DISCUSS OUR IMAGE...'

"THIS, I AM TOLD, DOES NOT NECESSARILY MEAN WE WILL BE MOVING THE WHOLE WORKS TO KRAKOW!"

27

BORN AGAIN

'WHATYA MEAN, YOU'RE WAITING FOR HUMPHREY HAWKINS? I AM HUMPHREY HAWKINS!'

30

'I'VE DECIDED TO SUSPEND YOUR SENTENCE, FARBER — — YOU'RE FREE TO GO.   JUST DON'T WANDER
OFF TOO FAR!'

'STOP YELLING AT US, BOY! CAN'T YOU GET ANYTHING RIGHT?'

33

34

'TAKE A LOOK AT THE BOTTOM OF YOURS... MINE SAYS "SUBJECT TO RECALL"!'

36

37

TALLY-HO! -- A VIRGINIA HUNT SCENE

'ENJOY ALL THIS WHILE YOU CAN —— COMES THE DEEP DEPRESSION, WE'LL BE LOOKING BACK ON THESE AS THE GOOD OLD DAYS!'

39

'CERTAINLY HE NEEDS DENTURES — YOU'VE LET HIM WATCH TOO MANY
SUGAR-RICH JUNK-FOOD TV COMMERCIALS!'

'OK, MENAHEM, ANWAR —— LET'S RUN THROUGH THE DAM' THING ONCE MORE...'

'BLOODY MANIACS! THEY'LL GIVE US ALL A BAD NAME!'

42

43

'HOO'S ON FIRST? I-DONG-NO? NO, HEE'S ON THIRD...THEN, WAT'S ON SECOND...'

'THEY'RE NOT SUPPOSED TO ADVERTISE, BUT HE GAVE ME A SPECIAL RATE FOR PROMISING TO SHOW IT TO EVERYONE!'

'WE HOLD THESE TRUTHS TO BE SELF-EVIDENT! GOVERNMENT OF, BY AND FOR THE PEOPLE! THE CHINESE DREAM! WORSHIP OF YOUTH, KICK THE ELDERLY, THE SEX REVOLUTION, ROCK MUSIC, CHOLESTEROL, JIM JONES — WE GOT OUR RIGHTS!'

MEANWHILE, BACK ON THE GUIDELINES...

49

'STAND BACK OR I'LL BE FORCED TO TURN THESE LITTLE ANGELS LOOSE ON YOUR LOUSY, BROKEN-DOWN PUBLIC EDUCATION SYSTEM!'

BOAT PEOPLE

51

52

"OF COURSE, I'D RESIGN AT ONCE IF I THOUGHT FOR A MOMENT THEY REALLY MEANT IT!"

'TEDDY AND I HAVE A VERY GOOD RELATIONSHIP——I GET TO DO THE DIRTY WORK AND HE GETS TO RIDE UP THERE AND LOOK GOOD!'

EEK!

OLIPHANT

56

57

THE CHINA CARD

'WE HAVE SOME HIGHLY INCONVENIENT NEWS...'

'A LUMP OF COAL...??'

'...LIMITED TO AN ALTITUDE NOT HIGHER THAN TEN FEET NOR LOWER THAN AND INCLUDING ZERO FEET ABOVE THE GROUND AND NO CLOSER THAN FIVE HUNDRED MILES FROM ANY TERMINAL CONTROL AREA...'

65

'... AND HERE, WITH HIS ANNOUNCEMENT OF HIS DECISION TO GIVE UP SEX, AND HOW IT WILL AFFECT ALL OF YOU, IS SECRETARY CALIFANO!'

67

HIS BEST SHOT

'PAHLAVI, BAKHTIAR, KHOMEINI - SCHLOMEINI — WHERE THE HELL'S THE GAS PUMP?'

'WELL, ER, YES... WE ARE LOOKING FOR A PLACE TO STAY...'

72

'START PACKING OUR STUFF — — AFTER WATCHING AMERICAN TELEVISION PROGRAMS, MR. TENG IS READY TO GIVE THIS COUNTRY BACK TO TAIWAN!'

THE FIFTH HORSEMAN

74

'I TRIED TO EXPLAIN TO MR. TENG JUST HOW IT WORKS, BUT I DON'T KNOW IF HE GRASPED IT...'

76

'OF COURSE, THEY NEVER REALLY WERE OVERLY ENTHUSIASTIC ABOUT THE PASSENGER BUSINESS...'

79

'PERSONALLY, I AGREE WITH YOUR MOTHER — — SHE DOESN'T NEED IMMUNIZING AGAINST ANYTHING, AND JIMMY CARTER DOESN'T KNOW WHAT THE HELL HE'S TALKING ABOUT!'

'WHY, PANCHO, BABY, YOU SLY OL' FOX — — WE JUST HEARD ABOUT YOUR WIN IN THE WORLD OIL SWEEPSTAKES!'

'WELL, YOU JUST TELL HIM, LUCILLE, THAT BEING RUDE, UNFRIENDLY AND ARROGANT IS NO WAY TO TREAT THE HAVE-NOTS OF THIS WORLD!'

PENDING EMERGENCIES

ENERGY POLICY

GASOLINE RESTRICTIONS

THE DOLLAR

RE-ELECTION

PREDICTED RECESSION

'WHAT DOES IT ALL MEAN, CARRUTHERS? THE WORD IS ISSUED THAT ONLY ESSENTIAL FEDERAL EMPLOYEES NEED REPORT FOR WORK-- AND NOBODY SHOWS UP!'

'THE PLAN SAYS WE WAIT UNTIL HE DOZES OFF — — BUT HE NEVER DOZES OFF...'

...AND, WHAT IS WORSE, GUNNED DOWN BY A 'BROAD!'

'DON'T BORE ME WITH YOUR TROUBLES—— YOU HAVE MINE TO SOLVE FIRST!'

92

'HE SENT DOWN THESE REVISED COPIES FOR YOUR APPROVAL, MENACHEM....'

93

'EXCUSE ME, SISTERS—— IS THIS THE PLACE FOR THE BIG GALA
RIGHT-TO-PAY-ALIMONY VICTORY CELEBRATION BLAST?'

'IT WOULD SEEM THAT SOME SNIVELLING MALCONTENTS AMONG YOU HAVE BEEN COMPLAINING TO THEIR CONGRESSMEN ABOUT OUR COSTS AND SERVICES...'

97

THANK YOU, ALBERT EINSTEIN

'OF COURSE, WE WILL HAVE PROVISIONS IN THE FINAL DRAFT TO PROTECT YOU FROM EACH OTHER...'

WASHINGTON, 3.6 MILLION YEARS HENCE: ANTHROPOLOGISTS SAY FOSSILIZED FOOTPRINTS FOUND HERE ARE OF A LARGE CREATURE BEING FOLLOWED BY A SMALLER CREATURE WHO WAS POSSIBLY CARRYING SOMETHING.

'BILLY CARTER? THET NAME RING A BALE WITH YO' LEROY? CARTER PEANUT WAREHOUSE? WHAH, AH SEEMS TO PLUMB FERGIT WHAR THET IS, DON'T YO', LEROY? MEBBE THESE BOYS IN TH' WRONG TOWN...'

102

'I KEEP TELLING MYSELF...I'M NOT LOSING FIVE BILLION — — I'M GAINING A DEPENDENT!'

'DO YOU DO ANY SHOEING WORK?'

'I REPEAT—THERE IS NO REAL CAUSE FOR ALARM...'

'DO YOU THINK MR. RAFSHOON COULD HELP ME WITH MY IMAGE..?'

107

108

'HE SAYS HE WON'T GO IN WITHOUT SOME WRITTEN ASSURANCE THAT IT WON'T MAKE HIM STERILE!'

'KEEP LAUGHING AND TALKING -- IT DRIVES THEM CRAZY!'

110

'DIET?? WHO'S GOING ON A DIET?'

'SOMETIMES I THINK THIS WHOLE THING IS GETTING AWAY FROM ME!'

112

'WHAT A CON MAN! THAT TOURIST JERRY BROWN CALLED THIS A CATALYTIC DEVICE FOR ADDING MORE MEANINGFUL VIBES TO INTERPERSONAL RELATIONSHIPS .... BUT IT'S REALLY ONLY A JOINT!'

VERIFICATION

'WHO'S THIS SAINT HOWARD THE JARVIS THEY ALL KEEP PRAYING TO?'

SUPREME COURT PRESS LIBEL DECISION

MALICIOUS? TO DRAW PEOPLE LIKE BIRDIES??

'PRETTY SOON WE'LL HAVE THE PRESS TOO SCARED TO CRITICIZE ANYONE--INCLUDING US!'

117

PLANTED FOR
PEACE BY
ANWAR SADAT
MENAHEM BEGIN

ANOTHER FEARLESS ASSASSINATION

'I WONDERED WHERE OLD WHATSISNAME WAS HIDING OUT!'

'BUT IT'S ALL ITEMIZED, SIR—— THAT CHARGE THERE IS FOR OUR DESIGNING GOOF, THAT CHARGE IS FOR OUR SUBSEQUENT MALFUNCTION GOOF, THEN THERE'S THE HUMAN GOOF CHARGE, AND THE DISASTER CHARGE...'

THE WINDFALL MACHINE (Reg. U.S. Pat. Off.)

121

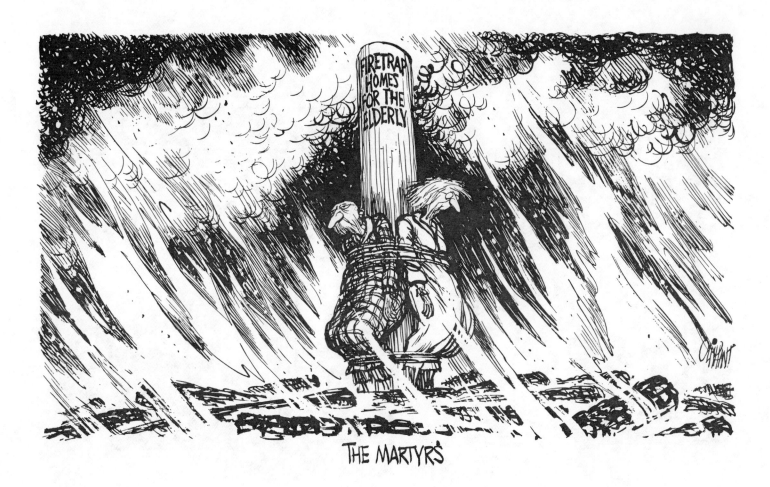

THE MARTYRS

THERE! A PART ON THE LEFT AND A NEW ME...RIGHT?

NO? WELL, HOW'S THIS FOR NICELY NON-COMMITTAL?

MAYBE STRAIGHT BACK— TOUGH, HUH?...NO?

THE CASUAL, WINDSWEPT ME... HE SAID WHAT? BALONEY!!

NICE, YUL

THAT ◎!!!?* KENNEDY!!

'SHE SEEMS LIKE THE MAN FOR THE JOB...'

THE TERRITORIAL IMPERATIVE

126

'YES, I STILL THINK THIS IS ALL A BIG OIL COMPANY HOAX ... QUITE A CONVINCING HOAX, MIND YOU, BUT A HOAX, NEVERTHELESS...'

'AW, JEEZ, JODY, DO I HAVE TO BE THE ANT? I MEAN, I UNDERSTAND THE MOTIVES OF THE PLAY, BUT PLAYING A GODDAM ANT...??'

130

'I LIKE TO COME OUT AND REVIEW THE TROOPS FROM TIME TO TIME... GIVE THEM A LITTLE PEP-TALK OR TWO, KEEP UP THEIR MORALE, STUFF LIKE THAT...'

'ALL THOSE OF YOU WHO WOULD NOT NORMALLY HAVE BEEN EXECUTED UNDER MY NEW LIBERAL POLICY OF MERCY ARE FREE TO GO!'

'ALL THE TECHNOLOGICAL ADVANCES OF COMPUTER SCIENCE IN RETURN FOR A SHIPLOAD OF DIM SIMS...AND JUANITA KREPS SAYS THE CHINESE HAVE TROUBLE UNDERSTANDING COMPLICATED TRADE AGREEMENTS!'

'WELL, I SUPPOSE WE'LL HAVE TO DISREGARD OUR EARLIER COMPUTATIONS...'

THIS IS NO TIME FOR HUMAN RIGHTS-- RIGHT?

OIL

FOR U.S.

'(GULP) WAIT, MR. KHOMEINI, SIR! PAY NO ATTENTION TO MY SILLY CRITICISM--AFTER ALL, WHO YOU EXECUTE IS YOUR BUSINESS, RIGHT?...RIGHT!'

'HELLO--WHO'S THERE? Y'ALL COME IN... GOLLY, I HOPE IT'S GOOD NEWS FOR A CHANGE!'

'WHO'S THE WET BLANKET?'

'IF ONLY THERE HAD BEEN A PRIVATE LIGHT AIRCRAFT INVOLVED WHICH WE COULD BLAME FOR ALL THIS ... BUT THIS TIME, GOD FORBID, THERE'S NO-ONE TO BLAME BUT US!'

'IF WE DON'T CATCH YOU, YOU'LL <u>WHAT</u>?   YOU CAN'T THREATEN US -- AND WE'VE GOT A RULING FROM A JUDGE, SAYING <u>JUST</u> THAT! MAYBE YOU COULD WRITE YOUR CONGRESSMAN, HA, HA ...'

'UNTIL YESTERDAY I WAS A SIMPLE CLERK (SECOND CLASS) IN THE POLISH PEOPLE'S ENTRY-VISA APPROVALS OFFICE --HOW WAS I TO KNOW WHO KAROL WOJTYLA OF CRACOW REALLY IS?'

143

144

'NICE TRY, SHAH!'

'KEEP YOUR HEAD DOWN -- THESE SWAMPS ARE FULL OF COMMUNISTS!'

147

'I'M BEGINNING TO UNDERSTAND WHY ALL YOU AMERICANS MISS JOHN WAYNE SO MUCH!'

THE MISSIONARY

'NOW AN' DEN DEY GOTTA BE REMINDED JUST WHO IS RUNNIN' DIS COUNTRY...'

151

'BIG OIL WANTED US TO DROP BY AND RUIN DA REST OF YOUR SUMMER BY INFORMIN' YOUS OF OUR EXTORTION PLANS FOR DA COMIN' WINTER!'

155

"'AND JUST HOW,' LAUGHED THE OPEC MEMBERS, 'DO A GRUBBY BUNCH OF INFIDEL PIG MACHINISTS PLAN TO THREATEN OUR MIGHTY CARTEL?' SO WE DID SOME MACHINING ON ONE SIDE OF ALL THEIR CAMELS!"

'NO GAS, NO FUEL OIL, NO ENERGY, NO ECONOMY, NO LEADERS, NO TRUCKERS, NO FOOD —— NOW _THIS_??'

GROMYKO

BAKER

158

THE BURGER COURT AT WORK

THE LONG, COLD SUMMER

BOAT PEOPLE

'DO COME ON OUT, HONEY -- THE NICE MAN FROM NASA SAYS THERE'S MORE CHANCE YOU'LL BE HIT BY A DC-10 THAN BY SKYLAB, AND THE NICE MAN FROM THE FAA SAYS THAT THE DC-10 IS QUITE SAFE AGAIN...'

SUDDENLY, CAPTAIN CARTER FELT THE URGENT NEED TO TAKE COMMAND!

'AH, YES, SENORITA SANDINISTA, HOW BEAUTIFUL YOU ARE WHEN YOU'RE ANGRY, YES, INDEED! HIM?
OH, A SMALL LIBATION OR TWO, TOGETHER. HARDLY KNOW THE SCOUNDREL...AH, MAY I COME IN..?'

'WHY, IT'S MR. MOSES AND COMPANY, BACK FROM THE MOUNTAIN ... WHAT'S THE GOOD WORD, MOSE?'

167

'HENRY — IT'S THE THERMOSTAT POLICE!'

168

'NOW WHO SAYS WE DON'T HAVE ANY LEADERS — RIGHT, HAM?'

YOU'D HAVE BEEN PROUD OF ME TODAY, ROSALYNN!

I USED MY NEW, FORCEFUL MANNER TO CHEW OUT ANDY YOUNG!

BOY, DID I RIP INTO HIM! I TORE HIM UP ONE SIDE AN' DOWN THE OTHER !!!

I TOLD HIM HE'D BEEN AN EMBARRASSMENT TO ME AND THIS ADMINISTRATION TOO MANY TIMES! SHAPE UP OR SHIP OUT!!

OLIPHANT

I REALLY GAVE HIM HELL!

OF COURSE, I DID APOLOGIZE STRAIGHT AWAY. I DON'T THINK HE'S TOO ANGRY WITH ME BECAUSE OF IT. I DO HOPE HE'LL STAY WITH THE BRAVE NEW CABINET. DID I DO THE RIGHT THING...?

DID AND UN-DID

171

'JIMMY! THERE'S AN ARTICLE HEAH CALLIN' Y'ALL ARROGANT, IGNORANT, SPITEFUL, COMPLACENT AND INSECU....FUNNY--HE'ALL WAS HERE JES' A MINUTE AGO!'

173

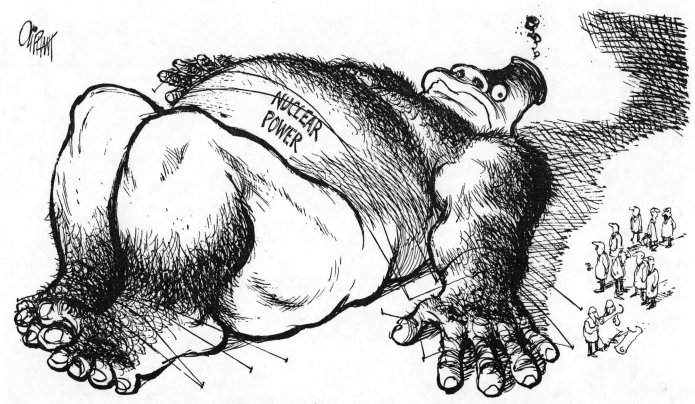

EVERYTHING IS UNDER CONTROL

'WELL, I REMEMBER SWIMMING IN THE POND... AND I REMEMBER LOOKING UP AND SEEING THIS SCREAMING MONSTER WITH HUGE RABBIT TEETH COMING AT ME WITH A CANOE PADDLE... BUT THE REST IS A BLANK.'

'I DOUBT IT, CARSTAIRS — IF THEY WERE SOVIET COMBAT TROOPS, WOULDN'T WE HAVE SPOTTED THEM AGES AGO?'

'I'LL BET TEDDY DOESN'T TALK LIKE THAT TO <u>HIS</u> MOTHER WHEN SHE TRIES TO HELP!'

'TAKE MY MONEY, TAKE MY NAME, TAKE MY INTEGRITY, TAKE MY SELF-RESPECT, TAKE ANYTHING —BUT PLEASE LEAVE ME MY SALT TREATY!'

SPEAKING OF INFALLIBILITY...

'I DON'T KNOW WHY WE HAD TO IMPORT A POPE WHEN WE HAVE ME!'

181

SEN. HERMAN E. TALMADGE AFTER BEING DENOUNCED BY THE SENATE.

THE SENATE AFTER DENOUNCING SENATOR TALMADGE.

'I'M WORRIED—THIS GROUP COULD MAKE THAT JOKER INSIDE LOOK HALF-WAY GOOD!'

`I THINK HELP IS ON THE WAY... IT BEING CAMPAIGN TIME.'

'HEY, I CAN'T STAND SEEING THE POOR AND THE ELDERLY STAND THERE AND FREEZE THROUGH THE WINTER—HAVE THE BOYS GO OUT AND ROUGH THEM UP A LITTLE!'

186

'AH, YES! WHAT WILL THE AMUSING LITTLE CHAP THINK OF NEXT? LUCKILY FOR HIM, I NEVER PANIC IN A CRISIS, OTHERWISE I'D BE TEMPTED TO STOMP THE HELL OUT OF HIM, YES, INDEED!'

'SO, ONCE UPON A TIME HE WENT ON TV, AND HE LIED TO THE PEOPLE ... SO, WHAT'S WRONG WITH THAT?'

'ACTUALLY, I LOOK UPON IT AS A <u>GOOD</u> OMEN... Y'ALL ARE GOING TO END UP WITH A BOATLOAD OF RATS!'

'FOR THE BENEFIT OF THOSE OF YOU WHO MAY NOT HAVE HEARD ME THE FIRST TIME, I HEREBY ANNOUNCE...

'OOPS!'

'THERE Y'GO, OL' BUDDY — I PROMISE THAT WHEN I GET MY INHERITANCE FROM UNCLE, YOU GET HALF!'

'WHY DO THEY NEVER ATTACK SOVIET EMBASSIES? AH, COMRADE, IS BECAUSE THEY KNOW
WE DO NOT ALLOW SUCH THINGS.'

196

'HENRY SAYS UNLESS SOMEONE APOLOGIZES FOR CALLING HIM ALL THOSE NASTY NAMES, HE'S GOING TO HOLD HIS BREATH TILL HE TURNS BLUE, AND THEN TAKE HIS BALL AND GO HOME!'

198

'HI, THERE! PARDON MY APPEARANCE, BUT I WANT TO DISCUSS WITH YOU THE LACK OF LEADERSHIP IN THIS COUNTRY.'